A Rookie reader®

Shadows

Written by Deanna Calvert
Illustrated by Mike Lester

Children's Press®
A Division of Scholastic Inc.
New York • Toronto • London • Auckland • Sydney
Mexico City • New Delhi • Hong Kong
Danbury, Connecticut

To Carolyn, my joy and inspiration, and to Kyle, my best friend. Without them, my shadow would mope.
—D.C.

To Robyn, my hero
—M.L.

Reading Consultants

Linda Cornwell
Literacy Specialist

Katharine A. Kane
Education Consultant
(Retired, San Diego County Office of Education
and San Diego State University)

Library of Congress Cataloging-in-Publication Data
Calvert, Deanna.
　Shadows / written by Deanna Calvert ; illustrated by Mike Lester.
　　p. cm. — (A rookie reader)
Summary: Children teach their shadows to do everything the children can do.
　ISBN 0-516-23444-7 (lib. bdg.)　　　　0-516-25840-0 (pbk.)
　[1. Shadows—Fiction. 2. Stories in rhyme.] I. Lester, Mike, ill. II. Title. III. Series.
　PZ8.3.C1373Sh 2003
　[E]–dc21

　　　　　　　　　　　　　　　　2003007114

CHILDREN'S PRESS, and A ROOKIE READER®, and associated logos are trademarks and or
registered trademarks of Scholastic Library Publishing. SCHOLASTIC and associated logos are
trademarks and or registered trademarks of Scholastic Inc.
1 2 3 4 5 6 7 8 9 10 R 13 12 11 10 09 08 07 06 05 04

Shadows can box.

Shadows can catch.

Shadows can kick.
Shadows can scratch.

Shadows can fly.

Shadows can chase.

Shadows can jump.
Shadows can race.

13

Shadows can bend.

Shadows can skip.

Shadows can dance.
Shadows can trip.

Shadows can reach.
Shadows can bow.

They are easy to teach.
Just show them how.

Word List (25 words)

are	dance	race	them
bend	easy	reach	they
bow	fly	scratch	to
box	how	shadows	trip
can	jump	show	
catch	just	skip	
chase	kick	teach	

About the Author

Deanna Calvert lives in Birmingham, Alabama, with her husband, daughter, dog, and cat. She used to teach college writing and literature courses, but now writes full time for children. Besides writing and spending time with her family, she enjoys fresh air and blue skies, trips to the zoo, and any kind of travel.

About the Illustrator

Mike Lester has been a professional artist, illustrator, and writer for twenty years. He was born and raised in Atlanta, Georgia, and graduated with a degree in Graphic Design from the University of Georgia. He has created images for ad campaigns and national magazines, along with illustrating numerous children's books, games, and products.